A MODERN NERD'S GUIDE TO
FAN FICTION

BY KATIE KAWA

 Gareth Stevens
PUBLISHING

Please visit our website, www.garethstevens.com. For a free color catalog of all our high-quality books, call toll free 1-800-542-2595 or fax 1-877-542-2596.

Cataloging-in-Publication Data

Names: Kawa, Katie.
Title: A modern nerd's guide to fan fiction / Katie Kawa.
Description: New York : Gareth Stevens Publishing, 2020. | Series: Geek out! | Includes glossary and index.
Identifiers: ISBN 9781538240144 (pbk.) | ISBN 9781538240168 (library bound) | ISBN 9781538240151 (6 pack)
Subjects: LCSH: Fan fiction–Authorship–Juvenile literature. | Fan fiction–History and criticism–Juvenile literature.
Classification: LCC PN3377.5.F33 K39 2020 | DDC 808.3–dc23

First Edition

Published in 2020 by
Gareth Stevens Publishing
111 East 14th Street, Suite 349
New York, NY 10003

Copyright © 2020 Gareth Stevens Publishing

Designer: Sarah Liddell
Editor: Abby Badach Doyle

Photo credits: Cover, pp. 1, 23 Monkey Business Images/Shutterstock.com; texture used throughout StrelaStudio/Shutterstock.com; p. 5 Daniel Zuchnik/Contributor/Getty Images Entertainment/Getty Images; p. 7 Noam Galai/Contributor/WireImage/Getty Images; p. 8 Flamingo Images/Shutterstock.com; p. 9 Neilson Barnard/Staff/Getty Images Entertainment/Getty Images; p. 11 PYMCA/Contributor/Universal Images Group/Getty Images; p. 12 Sharaf Maksumov/Shutterstock.com; pp. 13, 19 wavebreakmedia/Shutterstock.com; p. 15 VGstockstudio/Shutterstock.com; p. 16 Sunset Boulevard/Contributor/Corbis Historical/Getty Images; p. 17 WeAre/Shutterstock.com; p. 22 Syda Productions/Shutterstock.com; p. 25 Prostock-studio/Shutterstock.com; p. 28 ANURAK PONGPATIMET/Shutterstock.com; p. 29 Johnny Louis/Contributor/FilmMagic/Getty Images.

Printed in the United States of America

CPSIA compliance information: Batch #CS19GS: For further information contact Gareth Stevens, New York, New York at 1-800-542-2595.

CONTENTS

Words in the glossary appear in **bold** type the first time they are used in the text.

WHAT IF?

What if Captain America and Wonder Woman were friends? What if the *Harry Potter* books ended differently? What if Ben Solo never became Kylo Ren in the *Star Wars* movies?

It can be fun to think about how you'd answer these kinds of questions about the books, movies, and TV shows you love. Some people have so much fun imagining these new stories that they write them down and share them with other fans. This kind of writing, which is created by fans but uses famous characters and settings, is called fan fiction. Keep reading to learn more about this popular part of fandom!

EVERY FAN IS DIFFERENT!

Some people have written hundreds of their own pieces of fan fiction, while other fan fiction writers have only written one story. Many fans don't write fan fiction at all. They only read other people's fan fiction, or they don't read any. Every fan is different, and they should all be treated with respect.

Many fan fiction writers and readers proudly call themselves nerds. A nerd, or geek, is someone who cares a lot about something, such as a book, movie, video game, or even a sports team!

5

NOTHING NEW

People have been writing fan fiction for hundreds of years! Some people argue that the famous British writer William Shakespeare wrote his own kind of fan fiction based on other writers' work. The earliest kinds of fan fiction were often meant to be shared with a wide audience.

The kind of fan fiction people read today, which is usually shared only with other fans, started to get popular in the late 1960s. At that time, fans of the TV show *Star Trek* began writing their own stories about the show's characters, which were published in fan magazines known as zines.

WHAT DO YOU CALL IT?

Fan fiction has been around for a long time, and it's gone by many different names throughout its history. Today, it's often written as "fanfiction," and it's sometimes shortened to "fanfic." Many writers and readers have made that even shorter and often call the stories they're reading "fics."

Most fan fiction authors today only write for fun, much like the early Star Trek fans did. However, some writers' fan fiction has been turned into famous plays, books, or movies!

7

IS IT LAWFUL?

Some creators don't like or agree with fan fiction. However, since most people don't profit from fan fiction, many creators don't get mad that people are using their characters to make new stories. Today, there are laws that didn't exist in Shakespeare's time about using other people's ideas as your own. These are called copyright laws. Some people have argued that fan fiction goes against these laws.

Most people, though, believe fan fiction isn't about stealing anyone's work to claim it as your own. It's about people **responding** to the original because they're inspired by it. They believe this makes sharing fan fiction legal, or allowed.

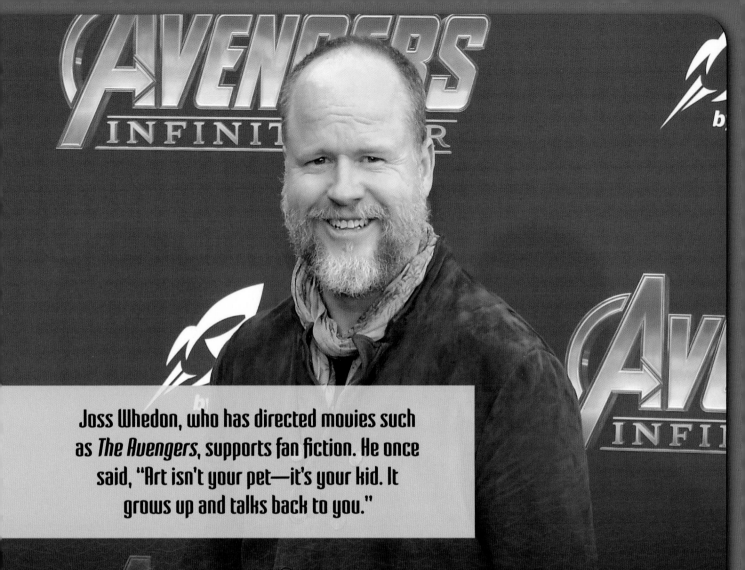

Joss Whedon, who has directed movies such as *The Avengers*, supports fan fiction. He once said, "Art isn't your pet—it's your kid. It grows up and talks back to you."

THEY'RE NOT MINE!

Some writers put a disclaimer at the beginning of their fics. A disclaimer is a formal way of saying, "These characters aren't mine!" The legal part of fan fiction can be confusing, so it's helpful to talk to a trusted adult about any questions you have.

A NEW POINT OF VIEW

Fan fiction uses familiar characters to tell new stories. Those stories often have a new point of view. Many fanfic writers take characters who were in the background of the original story and make them the main characters. They often do this with characters from groups who might not always get the spotlight, such as women.

In fan fiction, anyone can be the hero of a story. This kind of writing is about giving many different kinds of people a voice. Fanfic is written by men and women from many different races, backgrounds, and ages. In the world of fan fiction, everyone has a story to tell!

ALL LOVE STORIES ARE WELCOME

Fan fiction allows fans to create the love stories they want to see. In a popular kind of fic called slash, a male character falls in love with another male character. Many other fics feature two women falling in love. All kinds of love stories are welcome in the world of fanfic!

Fans don't look the same or come from the same background. They're all **unique**, and fan fiction is a way for them to tell their stories using characters they know and love.

FINDING FANFIC

Most fan fiction is posted online. There are more fics in the world than most people could read in a lifetime! One of the oldest and most popular fan fiction websites is FanFiction.net, which some people call "FF.net." Other popular websites for fan fiction are Archive of Our Own, Wattpad, and Tumblr.

These websites are all meant for users over 13 years old. On Archive of Our Own, you can ask your parent or guardian to post your fanfic for you. However, before you turn 13, you can still write fan fiction for yourself or to share with your friends and family!

Be a smart and safe fan! Always let a trusted adult know what you're doing online. Follow age rules on websites and only read fics that are rated for your age.

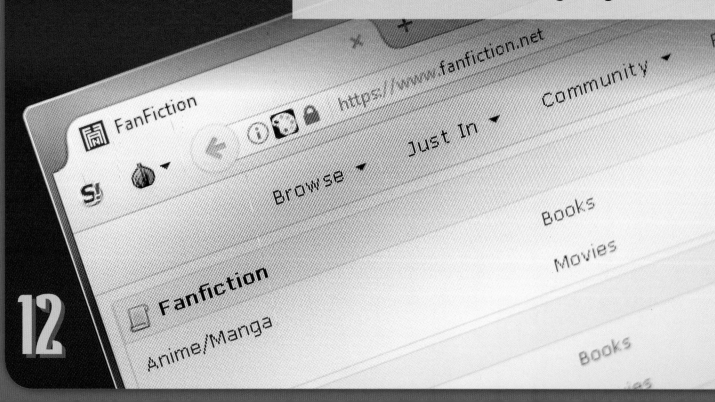

READING THE RATINGS

Most fics have ratings like movies to show which age groups should read them. Not all fanfic is **appropriate** for kids. Websites use different **symbols** for their ratings. For example, a fic that's appropriate for all ages is rated K on FanFiction.net, but it's rated G on Archive of Our Own.

WHAT'S YOUR STORY?

If you want to write your own fanfic, you need to decide what kind of story you want to tell. A good place to start is what's called a "missing moment" fic. It fills in the blanks in a story by imagining what might have happened in between the events shown in a book, movie, or TV show.

Other kinds of fanfic focus on the friendships between characters or on how one character is thinking or feeling during a moment from the original story. If these fics don't have a love story in them, they're called "gen fics" or "genfics."

THE REAL SIDE OF FANFIC

Some fans write fanfic about real people. In most cases, these fics are about famous people, such as actors, athletes, or members of a band. This kind of fanfic is known as Real Person Fiction (RPF). Some people feel uncomfortable about RPF, but most people know it's just for fun.

When you write fanfic, your imagination is the only limit! You can choose any character or person who inspires you to tell a new story.

RELATIONSHIP GOALS

Many fics are romances, or love stories. Some of the characters in these fics are in love in the original stories, but many aren't. Many fan fiction writers create romances between characters who are just friends, who dislike each other, or who've never spoken to each other! They like the idea of those characters falling in love, so they write about what that relationship might be like.

People who like the idea of two characters being in love are often called "shippers." They show their love for their favorite relationship, or "ship," in many ways, including writing and reading fan fiction.

A fan's favorite fictional couple is called an OTP, which stands for one true pairing. Many fans love to read fanfic about their OTP.

PRINCESS LEIA AND HAN SOLO FROM *STAR WARS*

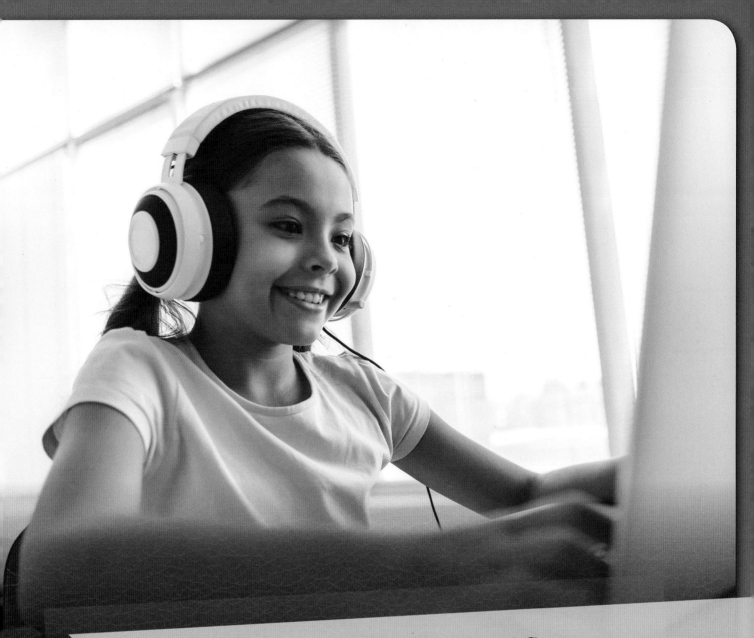

STORIES FROM SONGS

If you're stuck on an idea for a fanfic, listen to some of your favorite songs. Many people get inspiration for fanfic from music. Some writers even match the plot of their fanfic to the words of a song and put those words in the story. This is called a "songfic."

YOU CAN FIX IT!

Not all stories have a happy ending. If you're sad about the way a story ended, you can start writing a new one! "**Alternate** ending" fics imagine a new ending for a book, movie, or TV **episode**. In many cases, these endings are happier than the original ending and feature the writer's ship living happily ever after.

Fixing things you don't like about a story is a great way to start writing fanfic. This is called "fix-it fic." For example, if a character you love died in the original story, you can write a fic where they're alive and happy.

CREATE YOUR OWN CHARACTER

Sometimes, writers add new characters to their fics that weren't in the original stories. These are called original characters, or OCs. In some cases, writers create OCs who are a lot like them because they want to pretend that they're in the story. Creating an OC is a great way to make your fanfic even more unique!

Fans sometimes write fix-it fics that imagine a whole new season of a TV show if the show ended in a way that made them sad.

19

CREATING A NEW UNIVERSE

Some fanfic writers go one big step past writing an alternate ending and write an entire alternate universe! The universe is the world around the characters. Alternate universe fics change this part of the story in a major way. Many alternate universe, or AU, fics change the setting but keep the characters basically the same, such as putting the Harry Potter characters in a regular school.

Some AU fan fic imagines what it would be like if a male character was female or if a female character was male. For example, some AU fics feature a female Captain America!

COOL CROSSOVERS

One fun kind of AU fanfic to read and write is a crossover. In a crossover fanfic, characters from different stories meet each other and often go on an adventure together. Would you like to see Spider-Man and The Flash fighting bad guys together? You could write that crossover!

CHOOSE YOUR AU:

- CROSSOVER
- HIGH SCHOOL
- DIFFERENT TIME PERIOD
- FAIRY TALE
- PIRATES
- ATHLETES
- ROCK STARS
- COFFEE SHOP
- FAKE DATING

If you want to write an AU fanfic, these are some ideas to start thinking about. What if the story took place in a different time period? What if the characters were pirates, rock stars, or athletes? What if your OTP met at a coffee shop or had to pretend they were dating? You can write AU fics that answer these questions and more!

THE NEXT STEP

Once you decide what kind of fanfic you want to write, the next step is to plan how long your fic will be. Some fics are very short. Others are longer than the book they're based on!

Writers often break their fics up into chapters. Some writers post a chapter every week, but other writers post them whenever they have time. If a writer wants to post their whole fic at once, that's called a "one shot" or a "standalone." One shots don't have to be written all at once. You can take as much time as you need to write your fic.

You can write your fic in a notebook, on a computer, a tablet, or even a smartphone. Those **details** don't matter as much. The important thing is you start writing!

SHORT AND SWEET

When you first start writing fanfic, it's a good idea to start small. A "drabble" is a fanfic that's exactly 100 words. Writing drabbles is a fun way to work on your writing skills before you try a longer fic. Drabbles teach you to make every word count!

TIME TO WRITE!

Now, it's time to write! If you're still having trouble deciding what to write, you can ask your friends for prompts, which are ideas for fics. Every writer is different, so every writer will have a different writing process. Some people make an outline first. Others just start writing!

Your fic can look like a story, but it can also look like a play or a poem. It can have a lot of **dialogue**, or it can have none. Also, make sure to use your best writing skills. Even though fanfic isn't for a grade, good spelling and **grammar** are still important.

BEING A BETA

Many fanfic writers use a beta reader, or "beta." This person reads a fic before anyone else and makes sure it has proper spelling and grammar. They also tell you if the story makes sense. A friend or family member can be your beta, or you can be one for someone else.

Writing isn't always easy. It can help to read or watch parts of what you're basing your fic on to get all the details right. If it gets tough... keep writing!

25

SHARING YOUR STORY

Once you've finished writing your fanfic, read it from start to finish to make sure it's exactly what you want it to be. You can then choose to share it with others or keep it to yourself. Do whatever feels right for you!

When you get old enough to read and share fanfic online, you can leave **comments** on other people's fanfic, and they can leave comments on yours. It's important to be respectful when commenting on someone else's writing. Every writer works hard on their fanfic, so it's good manners to be kind to other fans.

OTHER KINDS OF WRITING

Fan fiction isn't the only kind of writing fans can do. Some fans write reviews of books, movies, TV episodes, or music. Other fans write **essays**—often called "meta"—**analyzing** stories or characters and talking about why they're important. These kinds of fan writing are also an important part of any fandom.

THE LANGUAGE OF FANFIC

A/N: THIS STANDS FOR "AUTHOR'S NOTE," WHICH IS A PLACE WHERE A FANFIC WRITER CAN WRITE DIRECTLY TO THEIR AUDIENCE ABOUT THEIR STORY OR THE PROCESS OF WRITING IT.

ANGST: A SAD FANFIC.

CANON: THE ORIGINAL SOURCE MATERIAL FOR A FANFIC, SUCH AS THE *STAR WARS* MOVIES.

FLUFF: A HAPPY FANFIC.

HEADCANON: AN IDEA A PERSON HAS ABOUT A CHARACTER THAT ISN'T OFFICIALLY INCLUDED IN CANON. HEADCANONS ARE OFTEN INSPIRATIONS FOR FANFIC.

HURT/COMFORT: A KIND OF FANFIC IN WHICH A CHARACTER GETS HURT AND ANOTHER CHARACTER TAKES CARE OF THEM.

MARY SUE (OR GARY STU): AN ORIGINAL CHARACTER WHO STANDS IN FOR THE AUTHOR AND IS OFTEN WRITTEN AS BEING PERFECT.

WIP: A WORK IN PROGRESS, WHICH IS A FANFIC POSTED IN CHAPTERS THAT HASN'T BEEN FINISHED YET.

The world of fanfic has its own kind of language! These are some popular terms that are used often on the big fanfic websites.

A FANFIC WRITER'S FUTURE

If you love reading and writing, fan fiction is the perfect way for you to have fun as a fan. You can find fanfic written about almost every story ever told. If you can't find a fic about your favorite character or ship . . . you can write your own!

Writing fan fiction is great practice for writing in school or for a career as a writer. Being a beta reader can help you sharpen your spelling and grammar skills if you want to be an editor when you grow up. Some famous writers started out writing fanfic. Maybe you can follow in their nerdy footsteps!

People of all ages write fanfic. Many popular fanfic writers have been creating their own stories since they were kids!

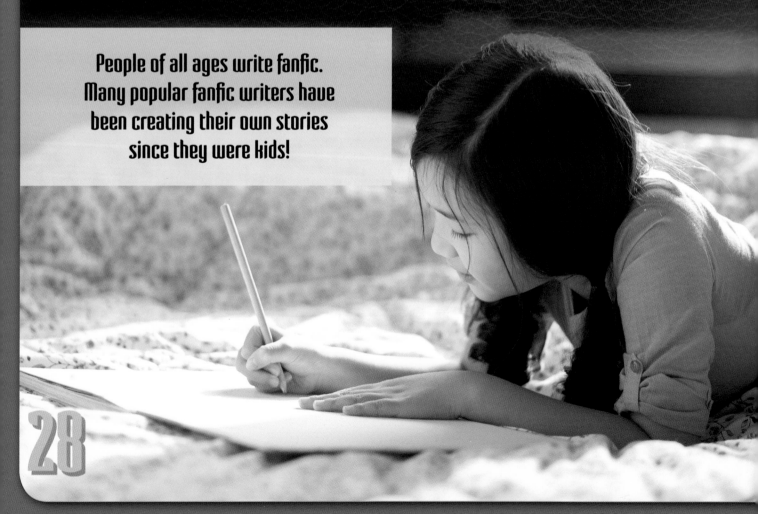

MEG CABOT

AN AUTHOR'S THOUGHTS

Meg Cabot, writer of the popular
Princess Diaries series and many other
books, wrote *Star Wars* fan fiction when
she was younger. She believes fan fiction
serves an important purpose. She wrote
on her website, "Writing fan fiction is
a good way for new writers to learn to
tell a story."

GLOSSARY

alternate: other than usual or traditional

analyze: to study something closely and carefully

appropriate: right for a certain kind of person or situation

comment: a statement of opinion about something. Also, to make a statement of opinion about something.

detail: a small part of something

dialogue: the things that are said by characters in a story, movie, or play

episode: a television show that is one part of a series

essay: a piece of writing that tells a person's thoughts or opinions about a subject

grammar: the rules of how words are used in a language

respond: to do something as a reaction to something that has happened

symbol: a picture, shape, or object that stands for something else

unique: one of a kind

FOR MORE INFORMATION

BOOKS

Anderson, Jennifer Joline. *Writing Fantastic Fiction*. Minneapolis, MN: Lerner Publishing Group, 2016.

DiPiazza, Francesca Davis. *Fandom: Fic Writers, Vidders, Gamers, Artists, and Cosplayers*. Minneapolis, MN: Twenty-First Century Books, 2018.

Stressless Homeschool. *Middle School Fan Fiction Writing Prompts: 30 Prompts to Jump Start Writing Projects Suitable for All Ages*. Scotts Valley, CA: CreateSpace Independent Publishing Platform, 2018.

WEBSITES

BrainPOP: Digital Etiquette
www.brainpop.com/technology/freemovies/digitaletiquette/
The short movie on this website teaches viewers about the importance of being respectful and clear online, which often becomes an issue in fanfic comments.

Kids' Rules for Online Safety
www.safekids.com/kids-rules-for-online-safety/
Fan fiction is often shared online, and this website features important online safety tips kids should know before visiting any websites, including fan fiction websites.

Meg's Blog: Fan Fiction
www.megcabot.com/2006/03/114184067156643148/
Readers who want to know more about Meg Cabot's history as a fan fiction writer and her thoughts on fanfic can check out this entry in the blog section of her official website.

INDEX